Network and Technology Questions from RIA firms that raise immediate...

...RED FLAGS!

Backups, Disaster Recovery, IT Compliance, and Cyber Security

By

Richard Mabbun

Julian Makas

ĪTEGRIA™

Taking RIA Technology to a Higher Level

DISCLAIMER: This book details the author's personal experiences with and opinions about regulatory compliance, SEC procedures, financial advisor business practices, network infrastructure design. The author is not licensed as an attorney, paralegal, financial advisor, regulatory auditor, or compliance officer.

The author and publisher are providing this book and its contents on an "as is" basis and make no representations or warranties of any kind with respect to this book or its contents. The author and publisher disclaim all such representations and warranties, including for example warranties of merchantability and educational or financial and/or regulatory advice for a particular purpose. In addition, the author and publisher do not represent or warrant that the information accessible via this book is accurate, complete or current.

Please consult with your own compliance attorney or financial practices professional regarding the suggestions and recommendations involving regulatory compliance information made in this book.

Except as specifically stated in this book, neither the author or publisher, nor any authors, contributors, or other representatives will be liable for damages arising out of or in connection with the use of this book. This is a comprehensive limitation of liability that applies to all damages of any kind, including (without limitation) compensatory; direct, indirect or consequential damages; loss of data, income or profit; loss of or damage to property and claims of third parties.

You understand that this book is not intended as a substitute for consultation with an attorney, financial practices professional or accounting professional. Before you begin any change in your business practices in any way, you should consult with a licensed professional to ensure that you are doing what's best for your situation.

This book provides content related to computer network and infrastructure design and best practices. As such, use of this book implies your acceptance of this disclaimer.

Table of Contents

5

I. Introduction

We, Richard Mabbun and Julian Makas, want to sincerely thank you for taking the time to review this book. We hope that the advice and insights we've placed here gained over our many years providing technology service to RIA firms, will be beneficial to your practice. We would also like to introduce you to our technology firm, ĪTEGRIA™, LLC, first so we can explain why we serve Registered Investment Advisors (RIA) exclusively; and second so that you as an RIA professional can understand the premise behind these "questions" and why they are such critical red flags to your firm's technology and infrastructure.

ĪTEGRIA™ offers technology and security support services exclusively to RIA firms. We deliver specialized services and solutions to protect RIA businesses, because the fact is – the financial services sector is the cross section of industry that is most targeted by hackers. Since our focus in on this sector, we understand best the unique challenges and technology requirements facing investment advisors across the nation. Initially, when we began brainstorming what ĪTEGRIA™ would be; we saw a problem in the RIA industry with respect to IT support and services. We actually believe this problem is in IT support in general, but it was very evident in the IT support available to small to medium sized RIA firms in particular. The problem, as we saw it, is that IT support firms regardless of their business model (MSP, Break/Fix, Time and Material) were only really interested in the generic technologies every business needs in order to operate. Because of this, we believe that the vast majority of IT firms throughout the country are "generalist" firms that limited their scope of work and services to the general technologies that their clients must have in place to run a typical office. For an RIA firm, this means that a generalist IT firm would provide services to manage the typical elements of a network such as the network infrastructure, servers, workstations, laptops and printers. But there was little to no reliable support on the industry specific software products that a RIA needed to have in place to run their business. Moreover, even for the parts of the network that a generalist firm did support, there was little to no understanding of the regulatory requirement needs the RIA firm faces every day. Because of this, "generalist" firms provided no acceptance of any responsibility for providing technology solutions that met all the RIA firm's needs. There was no true responsibility and even less accountability for making sure that the RIA firm was technologically complete.

By contrast, if a RIA firm had an internal IT Department, then there would be an implied expectation that the IT Department not only manages and has a thorough grasp of the standard business technologies (i.e. network infrastructure, servers, workstations, laptops, printers, etc.) but that department would also need to develop a keen understanding of the required RIA specific software technologies that the firm uses to execute its business. The IT Department would also have to provide answers and deploy solutions to address compliance requirements of the firm, at least from a technological standpoint. That same IT Department would also of course be both responsible and accountable to the firm for all aspects of the business related to IT.

Unfortunately most small to medium sized RIA firms cannot afford to or have the desire to staff an entire IT Department of their own, so they had to rely on "generalist" IT firms that could at least provide them with a "vanilla network". They had to deal with support services that did not understand, or did not care to understand their industry specific software packages. Because of this, the IT firms would typically leave it up to the client to solve their own issues with vendors regarding these industry specific software packages. There was no accountability from IT to make sure everything was running for the RIA firm (network as well as software applications). And the responsibility for keeping this running was always left with the RIA firm who may not understand the needed technologies to keep the software working in the first place (hey, they are financial guys, not IT guys).

This is the problem ĪTEGRIA™ sought to solve by creating a company that is a "specialist" in the RIA industry. Our premise was to create an outsourced IT

Department for RIA firms that not only understood the general needs of the business, but was also able to understand the required regulatory aspects of the RIA industry. We worked closely with Compliance Consultants to determine what technologies a RIA needed to deploy to maintain regulatory compliance. We then began to really understand the most popular industry specific software packages that RIA firms required so that we can better understand how to solve problems that may come up with those packages. Working with the various software vendors, we find that we are able to solve software vendor specific issues because we are technologists speaking to their technologies. And so, ĪTEGRIA™ created a service model for RIA firms that would truly take responsibility and accountability for running their IT Department. We truly believe it is a service model that will revolutionize the way small and medium size RIA offices can operate their technology departments. When we take on the responsibility of protecting a small to medium size RIA firm, we are taking up a challenge to do something really incredible for that firm in the midst of an ever changing technology threat landscape.

Many small to medium size RIA firms have a false view that good service can only be achieved in large corporations with specialized IT departments that are geared to fight against all manner of threats to the corporation. At ĪTEGRIA™, we love technology and enjoy the challenges that technology provides, and we believe that technology and service should be done better for everyone, even smaller firms.

Bad service is easy to find, from your hometown hardware chain to the nationwide cable conglomerate. It has gotten to the point that what they call customer service is so terrible that you can hardly call it customer service at all. They don't exist to serve their customers; they exist to serve the company at which they work. When ĪTEGRIA™ came into existence, one of main goals was to amaze our customers at the level of true customer service we provide. When you partner with ĪTEGRIA™, a phone call to customer service gets you to connected with a person who knows both you and your company and is ready to help you without the usual 10 rounds of "did you turn on your PC?".

The price you pay for technological services should guarantee better results, even if you are a small to medium size business. We exist for these companies and deliver responsibility, accountability and a superior level of customer service. Now you know that the word 'serve' and 'service' are misused and convoluted in today's world; we feel we need to define it better because we want to provide real service. By real service we mean the kind of service that is being shown and proved all the time. It is service that is always taking care of your needs and making sure that everything is operating at its best. With this in mind, we define the excellent customer service that we promise to provide as **service in your best interest**. In addition, we deliver accountability and responsibility to the same level, in and for your best interest, because as you know the growth of your RIA business is the growth of our business. We are on board with you and your business.

Now that you know the core values of ĪTEGRIA™, responsibility, accountability, and service in your best interest, let's explore security. Security is highly specialized, very time and resource sensitive and this is where the implied unfair advantage for larger corporations enters the picture. In reality though, security is a necessity for firms of every size. Regardless of the size of your firm, you need security in the same way you need the internet in order to conduct business today. Often with small to medium size firms security seems like a necessity that is out of reach and that is where ĪTEGRIA™ comes in to fill that need.

Security is complicated and can be expensive. When you try to find the time to do the research on what your firm needs, you may find that even the research is so complex that you need an IT professional just to point out what is relevant to you and what is not. We find that what small to medium sized businesses need is a service model where the costs to deploy the proper technologies are distributed across the entire portfolio of clients. This will enable all RIA's, particularly small and medium-sized firms, the benefits of a true security team and offering at a proportionate cost to their business size. ĪTEGRIA™ provides its clients with exactly this comprehensive, detailed, and expert advice and service. It is the type of service you imagine in a corporation with 50,000 computers but not in a company with 10 computers.

At ĪTEGRIA™, we are changing that by offering network and technology assessments that showcases the technology and security needs unique to RIA firms. We have performed hundreds of assessments on RIA networks nationally from one-man operations to firms with 100+ employees and billions dollars in assets under management. We assess these networks in terms of technology best practices, regulatory requirements and best practices, and cyber-security awareness.

As you can imagine, we've seen all sorts of networks and technology practices. Some very good, and others that just make us cringe and wonder. We ask many questions in the assessment process, and given our experience, when we receive an answer that makes us cringe, it raises an immediate "Red Flag" for us to dig deeper into that part of review. That's the basis for this book. Here are some common "Red Flags". Are any of these present in your RIA firm?

II. Backups

As an RIA firm, backups and disaster recovery are functions of your network that are just as important as the design of the initial network infrastructure itself. Firms, large and small, spend a lot of time and money creating a network with the proper hardware and software, configuring the servers correctly and so on. During this time, rarely do these firms give as much thought to the recovery of the network and how they would recover their files, servers, and infrastructure should the need arise;

because of this, we feel that these networks are essentially incomplete without a backup and disaster recovery mechanism. This has been the case from the beginning, as far back as the 1950s and 1960s, when the media of choice for backups was magnetic tape. Backing up to tape meant you would store file-level backups daily to tape media, that tape media was stored onsite and once a day, week, or month a master copy would be rotated offsite. Since it was three levels of backup, restoration would take quite a while. At the same time, copies of the programs would be on diskettes (or later on CDs) stored offsite. If a server needed to be restored, it used to be quite an endeavor beginning with the operating system which had to be reinstalled, followed by the applications and programs which we also reinstalled, and then finally the data files were introduced from the backup tapes. At that point, the company could declare the server had been rebuilt.

Today's best practices for backup mechanisms still cover three levels of backup, a file-level, image or image-level and an offsite copy. Fortunately today we are able to take advantage of technology advances to make the process easier and faster. ITEGRIA's backup best practices have the three levels of backup being performed as follows: file-level backups should be done automatically using an online backup software which sends encrypted backup data to a Cloud Storage Facility or Data Center. At the Cloud, the files should be collected, encrypted, compressed and send to a second Data Centers. The second level of backup, are called image-level backups. Image-level backups are performed by programs like Acronis, Veeam or StorageCraft that take advantage of virtualization technologies and convert software copies of servers (called images) to files that can be copied to any storage device. These programs take image-level backups of both physical and virtual machines, store that into a file format, compress the data, encrypt it, and process it to data centers in the Cloud. Of course, the third level is automatically taken care of once you have copies of both file-level backups and image-level backups sent automatically to data centers. The data stored at the data centers is your third level of backup. In the case of a disaster, these files and images can be reconstituted into virtual machines; allowing you the ability to truly rebuild your server infrastructure in a Cloud environment. This is the methodology ITEGRIA performs as backups for our RIA clients and so we recommend this backup procedure to all our RIA firms because, as you can see, three levels of backup truly gives the RIA firm the tools needed to re-constitute a complete network infrastructure.

Now that you have the needed background information in mind, let's examine the red flag answers we hear to common questions when we ask potential clients about their backup procedures.

Red Flag - I backup to tape every night, isn't that enough?

While backing up to tape does, in fact, meet the minimum requirements for backup procedures, an RIA firm needs a more robust and recoverable backup mechanism to protect themselves, their clients, and their sensitive data. Here are the issues and risks associated with the tape backup methodology:

❖ **File-level Backups** – File-level backup programs only backup individual files. It does not create an image of either the physical or virtual machine that the program backs up. The problem, then arises, when a restore of a failed server needs to take place from these backups. File-level backups only backup data files – which means a restore of your server will require reloading the operating system of the servers, installing all the programs originally stored on that server, as well as restoring all the files from the backups. This restoration methodology is time consuming and also requires that every one of the required software application's install media be on hand to perform the restore. In the case of an Active Directory Server, this method will take a large amount of time; in addition, success rates are extremely low in comparison to other backup and restore techniques.

❖ **Magnetic Tape Media** – Invented back in 1928 in Germany by Fritz Pfleumer, the magnetic tape was used as a way to record and backup data as early as the 1950s. Compared to today's modern backup methods magnetic tapes have significant disadvantages that include:

- Magnetic tapes can be easily damaged either in the creation of the backup, in transit to an offsite location, and during the restoration process.

- Magnetic tapes are sensitive to temperature changes and must therefore be kept in a controlled environment with a temperature range between 65 degrees and 85 degrees Fahrenheit at all times.

- Magnetic Tapes are prone to the degradation of data over long periods of time even if kept at optimal conditions constantly.

❖ **The Rotation Schedule** – Tape backup methods lend themselves to manual human interventions. This means maintaining a rotating schedule to insure the tapes are changed out and taken offsite every day, which can lead to the potential for a great deal of human error.

While a tape backup regimen does perform file-level backups of the company's data on a daily basis; performing an image-level backup of an RIA firm's servers and having those image-level backups transmitted offsite automatically each night would be a considerably more efficient and dependable backup mechanism. Combining a file-level backup and an image-level backup mechanism that is then electronically taken offsite each night creates three levels of backups protecting you, your clients, and your RIA firm.

Red Flag - I backup to A USB device each night, won't that take care of it?

So you are successfully performing your backups on a nightly basis and storing into an external USB drive. These backups are then taken offsite nightly via the removable external USB drive. You may feel safe with this backup method, but in reality it does create risks to your company and your data (and your clients' data).

We'd like to suggest that if you choose this method, that the external USB drives you are using be "encrypted" drives so that they cannot be read by just anyone who happens to pick up the drive. After all the process of swapping out the external USB drives and transporting them to an offsite location is manual and requires a great deal of human intervention. During transportation the drive could be damaged or stolen and each of these scenarios places your firm at significant risk in the event of a disaster.

If your company's backup data is currently being stored on removable USB drives, your firm is at risk on multiple levels. First of all, while the backup is being performed, there is no central control over all the backup operations. This means if backups are performed daily, then a person must be responsible for ensuring that the backups actually occurred successfully each and every day on all the removable drives in use at any given time. Second, if the backups fail to be taken offsite daily, the firm is at risk. If an incident occurs at the company rendering the removable drives inoperable, restoration will be impossible. This brings us to the third instance, the fact that the external USB drives must be removed manually. Removing the drives and relocating them exposes them to damage, thus rendering the information completely inaccessible. Manually removing and relocating the drives offsite nightly exposes them to the possibility of being lost or stolen and all your data will go right along with it.

ITEGRIA™ recommends replacing the removable USB external hard drive backup mechanism with an automatic online backup system. This system will back up your data to remote data centers nightly without human intervention or any physical hardware involved. This results in your data, not only being backed up nightly, but also being offsite nightly and therefore making it accessible for restoration should your current network not be available. If the backup program used to perform these nightly backups can also create image-level backups, then that would be even better (per our three-levels of backup recommendation).

Red Flag - Isn't backup, disaster recovery, and records retention all the same thing?

Well, though they are related, they are not exactly the same thing. Backup and Disaster Recovery are functions that have to be built into your current network design and infrastructure. Everyone knows what backups are and why they are needed, whether they are doing it in the safest way possible or not. Disaster Recovery is exactly as it sounds; it is the process by which you resume your business following a disaster – a hurricane, flood, fire, computer virus or server crash. The problem with Disaster Recovery, coupled with the importance of Backups, is often overlooked because a disaster seems unlikely; but Backup and Disaster Recovery are requirements to maintain Business Continuity in the event of an actual disaster. Another way to think about it is that Disaster Recovery occurs after a significant event such as a flood, hurricane, terrorist threat, or any other catastrophe and is one of many steps in a Business Continuity Plan, which is specifically required by regulatory bodies and are the steps needed to maintain operation of your business during a significant event.

Records Retention is an RIA Compliance topic and is related to the length of time you are required to keep specific types of documents on hand. Back up and Disaster Recovery are both required in order to maintain Records Retention Compliance, but it can be more clearly understood as a method of safeguarding your Records Retention efforts. Records Retention policies, also known as Data Retention policies are vital for managing all your firm's data. Not only paper documentation, but the massive amounts of electronic data being managed in the digital age. If this data is not filed and stored properly it can lead to regulatory problems as well as operational issues. Consider all the data stored in your firm – customer related information, account information, financial records, sales data, investment records and so on – that you need to maintain in order to stay competitive in the market. Your records retention policy is essential, for without it you will not be capable of operating well or meeting regulatory requirements.

Red Flag - My IT company takes care of my backups, isn't that good enough?

Even if your IT Support firm promises to handle Backup and Disaster Recovery, your firm must know what levels of backups are being performed on a daily basis to support this function. You must know whether or not these daily backups are the most up-to-date mechanism for the security of all the data stored for your firm. Your firm must be aware if your backups are being transferred to an offsite facility on a daily basis. Another important point is whether or not your firm is receiving a report from your IT firm relating to the status of your day's backup job.

Remember, the best practices for backups cover three complete levels. The three levels are handled by file-level backups done offsite or to the Cloud. Image-level backups are performed by programs like Veeam, StorageCraft, or Acronis, which make an image-level backup of all your physical and virtual machines, storing, compressing, encrypting and processing to the Cloud data center. At that point level three is taken care of because both your file-level backup and image-level backups are being automatically sent to data centers, which then allow you the capability of completely rebuilding your server infrastructure should the need arise. This is the procedure used for backups for our RIA clients, and we highly recommend that you at least have some written procedure on file for how your current IT Support firm handles your backup. Make sure that it offers the three-levels of protection that your firm deserves, and make sure that there is a mechanism to report the daily occurrence of that backup process to you. Ideally this report can be sent to you via email or via a login portal. A printout of that report should be placed in your compliance manual on a regular basis as proof that the backups are occurring and that your firm is auditing it. At the end of the day, if you are unable to recover from data loss due to a disaster, it is your firm, not your IT Support firm that will suffer and have to deal with the repercussions. Not knowing the details of their backup methodology and leaving it 100% in the hands if your IT firm is an unnecessary risk for your RIA firm.

Red Flag - We've never tried restoring from our tape backups or USB drive backups, is that something we need to do?

The short answer yes – but why is it so important? You are probably thinking our backups are being performed on a nightly basis and stored into an external USB drive. This backup is then taken offsite on a nightly basis. This is good – well, a good start that is!

This process relies heavily on human intervention and in the manual process of swapping drives and taking them offsite any number of things could happen to your backed up data; it could be damaged in transit, stolen or lost altogether. We suggest that clients make sure that the external USB drives being used are 'encrypted' so that they cannot be read by just anyone. Your firm may already do this and again – we applaud your efforts, but what happens if you assume your need to do a system restore and discover you are unable to do so?

You need to realize the importance of knowing that your backups are working and that files can be restored in case of a system issue or a natural disaster. Your firm needs to have a backup testing policy in place that is done regularly, particularly following any system changes. Your firm needs to create a backup and restore scenario that can be tested systematically. Yes, this process can be costly, but the cost of not being able to recover lost data files or recover a downed server can be so much greater. Speak with your IT Support firm about performing periodic restores of your data from backup. Make sure that each time a user requests a file to be restored, that your IT Support firm is documenting the process and sending you a write-up to place in your compliance manual. You not only gain the much needed documentation, but also have documented that the restore procedure is sound.

III. Disaster Recovery

Disaster recovery is an important aspect of data security that is often misunderstood and confused with performing daily backups. Nobody likes to think that they will be a victim of a flood, hurricane, earthquake, fire, server crash, computer virus or other natural or man-made disaster; but the truth is – it does happen. Your firm needs to be protected in the event you do become a victim. How can you adequate prepare to recover your data or your entire infrastructure in the event of these types of disasters?

The solution to this dilemma is so vitally important to your business that the SEC requires a full disaster recovery test be performed and properly documented every single year to be in compliance with regulatory requirements. A major component of this disaster recovery test includes a test of the mechanism that will restore your firm's critical technology systems. Please note that this means that the annual disaster recovery test encompasses more than just the restoration of your technology systems. All this should be covered in your firm's Business Continuity Plan. With respect to this book, unless otherwise clarified, when discussing disaster recovery, we will concentrate our focus on the technology portion of that process.

ĪTEGRIA™ is constantly reviewing various backup methodologies to make sure that we deploy the best backup and disaster recovery methods for our RIA clients. The following are our best practices for backups and disaster recovery. Disaster recovery begins simply, with a reliable backup. As previously mentioned it is one of the most important functions performed by your system for your RIA firm. Your firm must be able to recover all your data and infrastructure in the event of a computer-effecting disaster. If your backup fails to function properly or your backup media fails, there will be no reliable disaster recovery of your data or your clients' data.

A good disaster recovery plan must be able to address a disaster at various levels. There are countless ways a disaster can affect your firm, and your disaster recovery plan and methodology needs to document how it will recover from various scenarios. There are disasters that affect an RIA firm strictly on a file-level basis. This can be as simple as someone accidentally deleting a client folder on a network drive, or as distressing as a computer being infected with the Crypto-Locker malware where the entire network files are maliciously encrypted, never to be accessed again. In this disaster scenario, a good file-level backup mechanism would be sufficient to recover from this disaster.

A second class of disaster has to do with the loss of an entire server at the firm's location. In this scenario for whatever reason, the entire server needs to be re-created from scratch. Examples of this scenario are a physical server losing its hard drive array, a physical server's operating system becomes corrupt for a variety of reasons and it will no longer boot up, a virtual machine server is damaged beyond repair, etc. All of these scenarios point to a server down situation. In this scenario, a good image-level backup mechanism becomes extremely critical to the disaster recovery process of a single server. Image-level backups are performed by specialized backup software mechanisms that take advantage of virtualization technologies to create the image "snapshots" of servers on at least on a daily basis. Software packages offered by Acronis, StorageCraft, and Veeam are very popular to perform these image-level backups but make sure that the software is part of a comprehensive and well thought-out backup storage system. These image-level backups can get very large if not properly thought out and used in combination with file-level backups as an overall disaster recovery plan. Keep in mind that in your planning process, if you have to re-create your downed server to new hardware all together, ask yourself where would that physical server come from? What are typical lead times for acquiring that hardware? If this is a virtual machine that has to be re-built, is there an existing virtual host server to load it into? If not, what arrangements do you need to make to acquire a new virtual host server? If a virtual host exists, will it have the needed resources to run the re-created server without disrupting the virtual machines currently running within the existing host? Can you see here that disaster recovery is so much more than backup software and performing the backups? Are you now recognizing that disaster recovery is more about planning and executing of the plans and processes you need to have in place?

A third level of disaster which you must consider is a disaster where there is a complete loss of your firm's capability to use or recover the existing network infrastructure. This type of disaster is more in line with catastrophic events such as natural disasters and acts of god (fire, hurricanes, tornados, floods, landslides, etc.) or political unrest and terrorism (domestic or international). Think of Hurricane Sandy in terms of natural disasters. Think of 9/11 in terms of man-made disasters. In either case, your firm must not only restore a file, or re-create a single or few servers; you need an entire network infrastructure and a means to access it from a different location other than your office space, which may no longer exist. In this ultimate level of disaster preparedness, it is important that two things are occurring with your daily backups for file-level and image-level. Backups must be automatically replicating to off-site datacenters that store the information in a secure and private space, and they must be transmitting the files in a secure and encrypted manner. Next, the data centers storing this information should have some way of replicating to a second, geographically diverse data center for redundancy. The data centers storage or "Cloud" providers must have the capability of accessing these backups both at a file and image-level and move them to an area where they can create a secure "private cloud" infrastructure. ĪTEGRIA™'s backup methodology allows for the re-creation of our client networks in this fashion using our Total AdvisorCloud™ network infrastructure. Having the capability to have your service provider recreate your network infrastructure in a private cloud using your most recent backups creates a virtual "hot-site" for your RIA firm. Once re-created, your firm should be able to use this virtual "hot-site" to operate your business until your local network infrastructure can be re-built or addressed. Keep in mind that for larger sized RIA firms, the performance of this virtual "hot-site" may not be as robust as their physical infrastructure, but it should have them working enough to conduct business. Those RIA firms that already use Private Cloud Providers to host their network infrastructure on a daily basis should have much of this methodology "baked" into their service offering. Make sure you totally understand your IT Support Firm's methodology for redundancy.

As you can see above, disaster recovery is about planning for and addressing continuity of your business processes at various disaster scenarios. Using backups at various levels is critical to that. Let's revisit again what backups you need and at what levels.

Backups should be performed at the three critical levels – file- level, image-level (also called server-level) and the cloud-level. Each level should be tested for reliability and recoverability on a regular schedule. At the file-level, all files should be backed up at least once per day, but preferably multiple times per day so that they can be restored in the event of a disaster. In the image-level back-up, a virtual copy of each server in your firm is made. Should a restore be required, your server can be restored from this image-level backup followed by restoration of your file-level backup. At the cloud-level all new file-level and image-level backups created daily should be uploaded to an offsite cloud data center and supply the ability to quickly and consistently restore your entire system in the event of a disaster. Having the capability to restore these backups and images to either a physical server or a virtual machine in a cloud environment is critical in the Disaster Recovery process and is what sets Disaster Recovery apart from the Backup process. If you do have daily offsite file-level and image-level backups, but there is no method or plan for you or your IT Support Company to re-build or re-create those files and images into a server then we would challenge you that your Disaster Recovery Plan is incomplete.

If you, your IT Support Company, or your firm does not have this as part of your plan, then make sure you schedule some time to work through the details. Once you have that written down, determine the best way to test it. It is only then that you can say that you have a Disaster Recovery Plan and not just a Backup Plan.

Red Flag – Disaster recovery? Didn't I just explain how we do our backups?

Ok so in the previous chapter and associated Red Flags, we discussed backups extensively. By now you should also know that backups are an essential component of a Disaster Recovery plan. And we've hinted to the fact that a Disaster Recovery plan and process are major components of an overall Business Continuity Plan.

The above Red Flag comes up often because many RIA firms assume that performing a backup every day constitutes a Disaster Recovery Plan. Sadly many IT Support firms position backup software and hardware packages as Backup and Disaster Recovery (BDR) mechanisms without truly examining every component of the solution they provide to see how it measures up in the three key disaster scenarios outlined in this chapter. Just having the software in place and performing backups does not guarantee that your firm can recover completely in the event of a disaster. Let's take a look at the common backup mechanisms and see what else need to consider before calling it a disaster recovery process.

File-Level Backup

The most common level of backups most firms have in place is file-level backups. There are numerous software packages that address file-level backups very well. When deployed correctly, file-level backups can be configured to perform backups multiple times per day to protect the firm from loss of any file or versions of files throughout the business day. Many of these file-level backup programs also allow for automatic encryption and transmission of the backup set to an off-site facility or on the "Cloud". ITEGRIA™'s best practices are to use an automatic online backup service to perform file-level backups that are automatically transmitted to "Cloud" data centers. We also suggest that the Cloud data center providers replicate that data to another distant data center to accomplish geographic diverse redundancy.

When thinking of file-level backup as a disaster recovery process, you will have to consider what types of scenarios will you be able to recover from and what resources will you need to have in place to facilitate that recovery. In a scenario where files were lost or corrupt, a file-level backup works perfectly to recover those missing files as long as the files are part of the backup set (or multiple backup sets) and you are restoring them within the retention period (number of days the oldest file is kept). In our second scenario where an entire server is lost and the files on that server are no longer accessible, then a file-level backup alone may fall short. In this scenario, in order to restore the server as well as the files within it, your firm would have to restore the server (either acquiring new hardware, fixing the existing one, or creating a new virtual machine), reload all the programs needed and that was on the original server, then perform a restore of all the files into the proper data directories and structure and according to the restore procedures of each software program. This process can be time consuming and depending on resources could take days or weeks to accomplish correctly.

Image-Level Backup

The second level of backup, the image-level, helps address backups of entire physical or virtual servers. Software companies such as Acronis, Veeam or StorageCraft are popular backup programs capable of image-level backups, and take advantage of virtualization technologies to create software copies of servers (called images) to files that can be copied to any storage device or media. Please note that image-level backups require a large amount of storage space, and best practices are to have a separate storage device (such as a Network Attached Storage – NAS) dedicated to these backup files. In many cases, the image-level backups can also serve as a file-level backup depending on the frequency that the image-level backups are created. Because of the amount of storage space needed, many times using this method of backup as a file-level backup will require many terabytes of data storage, and thus make using image-level backups as file-level backups cumbersome and expensive. Also administration of these backup processes tends to be more involved when having to deal with backup sets that occur multiple times per day.

Restoring a server from image-level backups is very reliable and typically very fast. If restoring a physical server, these images can be used to restore a server even if the new server and the old server are not exactly the same machinery (make, model, resources, etc.). This is a very attractive feature as many times finding the exact same hardware to restore a server may be problematical. These image-level backups can also be restored in a virtual machine as long as a virtual host server is present. Many times, as is the case with ITEGRIA™, your current IT provider or Cloud provider will have a virtual host server available for just these types of emergencies.

Please inquire with your IT provider if they have these capabilities so you can know what your options are in the event of a server loss. Part of disaster recovery planning is knowing what your firm must do when a restore needs to be done. If it means you know you must purchase a new server, then you must have an idea of the lead times of these servers. Then ask yourself is being down for the amount of time acceptable? If your IT provider has loaner servers available, then please make sure to ask them what the lead time are to deliver that server to your location or if they can restore your server on an impromptu "Cloud" network for quicker recovery times. You'll probably also want to know the terms of the loaner server with regard to costs and how long you can keep using the server. The key is to know exactly must happen when a server goes down and needs restoration. It's too late to find that out when you actually have a failure.

Cloud-Level Backup

Cloud- level or off-site level backups make up the third level of backups in ĪTEGRIA™'s best practices. This level of backup was designed to protect your RIA firm against any scenario where the onsite backup copies cannot be used to restore your files, servers or network infrastructure, and/or where your office network infrastructure cannot be accessed for whatever reason. A best practice for backups in general states that backups should be removed, either physically or electronically, from the office premises every night and a copy stored off-site. In the case of our two prior backup levels, this function should happen automatically as a feature of the software being used to create the backup. For example, online backup services that provide file-level backups automatically collect, compress, and encrypt the file-level data before sending it on to the "Cloud" data centers. This process will then automatically address at least part of the cloud-level or off-site level backup. The same holds true for most of the image-level backup programs. Once the image is done for that day, whether it is a full image or an incremental image, once the process is complete, then the program can be configured to copy that backup information in an encrypted fashion to an off-site

"Cloud" data center. This ensures that should a catastrophe happen to your firm's office space, then your data can be recreated from the file-level and image-level backups at the offsite or "Cloud" data centers.

But, just because your file-level and image-level backups are stored offsite in a "Cloud" data center does not mean that that data center or your IT provider has to means to use the facilities at the "Cloud" data center to re-create your network infrastructure. This is where you have to dig a bit deeper and work with your provider to see if they have the capability to use your cloud-level backups and create an impromptu "private cloud" network for your firm. This means they must provision a secured and separate network environment using the hardware and resources at the same data center where your backup data is stored. Your IT Support firm must then provision a way for your firm to access the re-created network environment so that you can continue to transact business in the event of a disaster.

By having a combination of the off-site or cloud-level storage of your backup files, and the capability to re-create your network environment in an impromptu "private cloud" using your backup data, your firm gains the ability to recovery from perhaps the most difficult scenario of disaster recovery. In determining the proper service providers and Cloud providers for this cloud-level backup, make sure you ask about what the provider does for redundancy of their systems, and how they deal with making sure that they are geographically diverse so that your environment can be restored in data centers outside your own geographic region.

Red Flag – I've never done a Disaster Recovery test, should I? How often?

Yes, you should perform a disaster recovery test on a regular basis, though no one likes to consider the possibility of the unthinkable disaster – fire, computer crash, hurricanes, and more do occur with more regularity than most of us would like to imagine.

Disaster Recovery should be managed by your current IT Support firm and they should be performing disaster recovery tests with regularity to insure that your data can be retrieved quickly and accurately in the event of an unforeseen disaster. It is important for the security of you and your firm, that this process is completely regularly, otherwise how will you know if it will work appropriately in a computer-catastrophe scenario.

Your disaster recovery protocol should be tested periodically throughout the year to ensure its viability should your data and system need to be restored. Regulatory bodies such as the SEC require that they be tested at least once per year. At the heart of your disaster recovery should be daily backups at the file-level and at the image- level. These backups must then be stored offsite daily, either physically or electronically. Backups should also be tested regularly for reliability and accuracy. If a disaster occurs and then your backup fails, disaster recovery for your firm will be virtually impossible to complete.

Once you are secure in the knowledge that your backups are working properly at both the file-level and image-level, a disaster recovery test should be done at least on an annual basis on a small portion of your data or a segment of test data to assure you that should your RIA firm experience a disaster, your clients' data as well as your own can be restored completely and without delay. A good way to do this is to go through the process of restoring a file server or an email server. The process of doing so will yield quite a number of lessons learned that must be addressed in the event of a true disaster. Ideally, a RIA firm should attempt to restore the entire network infrastructure once a year. The process of planning, executing, and documenting the recovery of the entire network infrastructure will be a very enlightening process for any RIA firm, and will highlight holes in your Disaster Recovery Plan with respect to your firm's technology that you probably never even considered. Review the three levels of backups and various disaster scenarios discussed in the last Red Flag and see how your firm would deal with those situations. This is a critical aspect of your business that we encourage every RIA to make a priority each year.

Red Flag- Isn't backup, disaster recovery, records retention and Business Continuity Planning all the same thing?

Well, the answer is "yes" and "no." While they are all closely related and tend to work hand-in-hand to keep your data secure, they are in fact different things. If this section may seem redundant with a Red Flag in the Backup chapter, it is because the question is relevant in both areas. But let's clarify it a bit more here…

Backup and Disaster Recovery

Backup and Disaster Recovery are necessary functions that should be built into your network design and should be prepared to help your firm maintain business continuity in the event that disaster strikes, whether it be fire, flood, computer virus or server crash. As addressed in previous sections, it is the use and deployment of proper tools and processes as well as planning to mitigate the risk of loss of data. In ĪTEGRIA™'s best practices, we encourage RIA firms to cover three levels of backups: file-level, image-level, and cloud-level. We also encourage RIA firms to consider at least three levels of disaster scenarios: file or data loss, server or local infrastructure loss, and building or work environment loss.

While many firms follow backup protocol by backing up at both the file-level and server- level, storing the backups offsite, either physically or electronically in the cloud; many do not create or practice disaster recovery protocol because they often feel that a disaster is completely unlikely or never went through the exercise of what to do in case of such an emergency. Well disasters do happen, very regularly, and could be something huge like a hurricane or flood, or something smaller like a server crash or a computer virus.

Disaster recovery protocol is what will help you resume business as usual after a troublesome event. It allows your system to be completely restored via your backups. When the protocol has been tested and practiced; disaster recovery can occur both quickly and accurately, getting your RIA firm back to business.

Records Retention

Records Retention is a compliance issue for RIA firms and is concerned with the length of time you are required to keep specific documents. Backup and Disaster Recovery must be in place in order for you to maintain and safeguard your Records Retention efforts.

Records Retention is an essential part of data management. Data, whether paper or electronic, must be stored and filed properly for both operational and regulatory requirements. Without a secure records retention protocol, your firm will not be able to meet regulatory compliance requirements.

Business Continuity Planning

Whereas backups and disaster recovery plans are technology steps taken so your firm knows how to *react* to a scenario, Business Continuity Planning (BCP) is a *proactive* exercise designed to mitigate the impact of a risk or disaster scenario. A BCP goes above and beyond addressing the firm's technology disaster recovery. It goes into planning for all aspects of the business and how they will function in the event of a disaster. Of course backup and disaster recovery are a huge part of a BCP, but BCP's also address questions such as who will be the person to contact the executive management team? Who will be responsible for contacting the clients and informing them of how you will continue servicing them? Will alternate offices be necessary, and if so, where has the firm already made arrangements? Who are all the pertinent vendors that must be notified, and what are all their contact numbers? The list goes not. While it is beyond the scope of this book to address everything a BCP should do, we bring it up here to illustrate that a Disaster Recovery Plan is part of the things addressed in the BCP.

IV. IT Compliance

IT Compliance is important for every RIA firm, including yours. On the same note, IT Compliance is challenging, even for the most savvy security and compliance specialists. Adhering to numerous regulations is an absolute necessity for your RIA firm, because compliance violations lead to a huge reduction in client confidence, not to mention the fines that accompany non-compliance. Given the fact that RIA firms are governed by several entities, depending on your offerings, it is important that you and your IT partner understand not only the IT requirements, but also the often every evolving regulatory environment.

Essentially, IT Compliance for RIA firms stems from following:

- Securities and Exchange Act of 1934 – rule 17a-3 – Records to be Made by certain Exchange Members, Brokers, and Dealers

- Securities and Exchange Act of 1934 – rule 17a-4 – Records to be Preserved by certain Exchange Members, Brokers and Dealers

- Various federal, state and local laws regarding data privacy and security

As much as possible, IT Compliance processes should be automated and feature a risk-based approach that protects information (yours and your clients), accesses and addresses potential threats with speed, while reducing both your costs and your risks. IT Compliance protocol must manage the expenses and labor audit and compliance requirements for your firm as well as create the IT policy and controls managing both your risk and your compliance. IT Compliance policies, along with needed controls, must then be implemented and enforced, plus have the ability to respond to management questions and IT auditors.

A well-rounded IT Compliance plan will include Data Security that protects your clients' personal and financial information. This type of information is a primary target for cyber-attacks and the appropriate level of data security assesses your firm's vulnerability and seals off potential breach points from cyber criminals. In addition, a comprehensive IT Compliance program will focus on data or records retention ensuring that documents, records and correspondence is handled appropriately, including document storage, data backup, and disaster recovery. IT Compliance review, data recovery and disaster recovery testing are inseparable and absolutely necessary for your firm to maintain client confidence and meet the regulatory requirements set forth by the governing entities.

Red Flag - I archive my email by just keeping a copy in my Outlook Mailbox, that's good right?

Unfortunately simply saving an email in your Inbox or a Labeled folder in your email program does not constitute a legitimate email archiving system. The SEC is very specific in 17a-4 as to the requirements of electronic data storage, and emails fall under that category. This is because there is always the chance that the email could be deleted or altered in some way. A true email archiving system prevents deletion and/or alteration from occurring by making an automated copy of the email and storing it a secure area. The copy cannot be altered, but can be scanned for specific keywords as necessary.

Also, depending on the type of email system and protocol you and your firm use, if the only copy of that email is in your Outlook Mailbox (or whatever email program you use), then if that PC failed and you lost all the data on the PC, your "archived"/ saved email would be lost as well.

A true email archiving system is necessary technology that should be in place in every RIA firm's network. It allows the firm to address necessary compliance and regulatory requirements regarding records and retention for emails that all RIA firms must address. Furthermore, a good email archiving services can aid the firm's Compliance Officer and Internal and External Audits in performing periodic supervisory review of both incoming and outgoing emails. These services offer a software platform that can even be configured to flag emails with specific keywords, again helping the supervisory review process. An email archive can also serve as another level of backup for your email system.

Red Flag - Our firm uses an onsite/local email archive, so we're compliant enough, aren't we?

If a local email archiving program is being used to perform the necessary role of email archiving for your firm, then, yes, the method used is adequate for the actual archiving portion as it is related to compliance. The problem we have discovered with this method is two-fold. First is that it makes it very difficult for the Compliance Officer to perform his or her supervisory review role. Second is that excellent backup and disaster recovery processes must be in place to ensure that the archive information is 100% recoverable and that no data can ever be lost. It is also important to have a way to purge old data (more than 5 years) from the archive that are no longer required to be stored according to rule 17a-4. Purging data from archives is something many RIA firms tend to overlook, but there have been occurrences of firms being "pinched" for compliance "findings" located in emails held longer than the required retention period.

With regard to the Compliance Officer being able to perform a periodic Supervisory Review of emails, most local email archive systems are little more than a database and records management applications. When Compliance Officers need to perform review, these archive programs are very cumbersome to navigate in order to extract the proper information from them. In contrast, an online email archiving service is designed not only to provide the archiving services; they are also designed to perform these Supervisory Review interfaces for Compliance Officers to perform their task. They are even able to generate the appropriate extract of emails in the proper format that most regulatory bodies require in an audit.

With respect to having an excellent backup and disaster recovery procedure (DRP) in place if you have a local email archiving system; the loss of an email archiving system and its data due to a poor DRP can be devastating to an RIA firm. In this scenario, the loss not only means the loss of important and timely internal and client communications, it also means that if asked to reproduce this information, your RIA firm would be unable to do so, thus creating a compliance "finding" or "event". This could mean hefty fines, and perhaps even worse, a loss of trust and damage to your reputation. An email archive service guards against this by offering an immediate offsite copy of all emails from and to your firm. In the event of a local disaster, the archive can also be used as a disaster recovery mechanism to restore emails in the local disaster.

Red Flag - We archive our mail in our CRM, so we have it taken care of, don't we?

Saving emails as a record in your RIA firm's Customer Relationship Management (CRM) may be a great way of keeping track of all touches with a particular client, but it does not constitute an email archiving system. Part of the prerequisites for an email archiving system is that the systems stores a copy of ALL inbound and outbound email in the ORIGINAL state it was sent or received. There can be no capability of altering the email. When saving emails into a CRM, many times the process to do this is by cutting and pasting portions or all of the email into the CRM as a record or a note. Other times there is a plugin from the CRM that can help this process along. However, at all times in this process, the original contents of the email can be altered, or omitted at the discretion of the person choosing to save the information. The fact that there are choices made by a person as to what gets saved and what does not eliminates the CRM as a true email archive system.

In addition, when regulatory bodies such as the U.S. Securities and Exchange Commission (SEC) comes to visit and asks you to produces a Personal Folder Storage (PST) file of all emails for a certain employee in a certain date range; pulling that information together and placing it in the appropriate format may prove difficult or impossible as the CRM was never designed to perform archiving tasks such as this. A true email archiving system or service handles these types of request very easily allowing your firm to produce the needed information quickly and accurately when needed.

V. Cyber Security

Cyber Security needs a focus driven approach in any size RIA firm. The data with which RIA's are entrusted is too valuable not to secure in the safest possible way. The management of Cyber Security standards should be backed by three guiding principles – responsibility, accountability and excellent service.

Cyber security today is necessary. It is a very specialized area that is both time and resource intensive, making many small and medium size RIA firms wonder if it is even possible for them to pull off the kind of security that is needed in this day and age. At first glance, it appears that only large firms are up to the task. After all they have the resources to hire a security officer, security staff, and install and monitor all the appropriate software, whereas a smaller firm may look at security and shrug their shoulders and ask, "…can we even afford this type of investment?" By its current perception, the cyber security industry seems to create an unfair advantage for larger corporations, but does it?

In all honesty cyber security is a necessity – to run the best RIA firm possible you need security in the same way that you need your Internet connection and the two must work hand in hand to keep your small to medium size RIA firm both trustworthy and competitive for your clientele. Why then does it seem so out of reach – so complicated and so costly?

Let's take a few minutes to review some of the most common red flags and misconceptions regarding cyber security we see in the small to medium size RIA industry. We will go over why some of these misunderstandings exists and how to empower yourself to think about and manage cyber security issues more appropriately within your firm.

Red Flag – We have a pretty stable network in place that should comply with common best practices, the next step would be a full blown security department and that doesn't seem to fit in with my firm's business goals. Isn't what I have in place good enough for what we do?

We are often asked how systems administration differs from cyber security and why smaller firms need to devote time and resources specifically to security. Most already work with an IT provider, or have an employee who seems to be keeping everything running smoothly. We commonly hear, "Sure we have some issues now and again, but overall everything appears stable and the network seems to be running by the book. As long as everything is set up the way it should be; we should be just fine." Properly administering your computers, networks and all the attached devices is paramount to having a functionally stable computing environment; but common systems administration alone barely scratches the surface regarding the functions and procedures that should be in place for creating a secure network.

System administration, or the role of a system administrator, tends to lean more toward the concepts of functionally, performance and availability. These functions, respectively, address the fact that the systems and network answer the functional needs of your business and its staff, do so in a performant manner, and have the stability and resilience to be available as needed. To attain these goals, general best practices must be applied. These best practices do bring aspects of security; however, a general administration implementation decision tends to gravitate towards the above mentioned concepts with much less emphasis on security. Moreover, general systems administration has a tendency to focus on the "problems" and major components of the network, such as servers, routers, etc. An "if it isn't broken, don't fix it" mentality tends to prevail; because, the focus is on functionally, performance and availability. Once these criteria have been met the goal becomes maintaining the status quo. While this may be acceptable for generalized system administration, rarely is this an acceptable methodology when security is considered.

Cyber Security must take a proactive stance with the understanding that your network environment is a living and ever changing entity that will move in and out of different states of secureness. Every new bug or vulnerability discovered along with every newly installed support software package and any added device creates an opportunity for a formally secure networking environment to become vulnerable to malicious attack. In this mindset, functionally, performance and availability are left to the devices of the systems administrators while the focus shifts to constantly monitoring for change and its ability to introduce weaknesses and vulnerabilities.

The amount of flexibility and change within an organization tends to be proportional to size. You asked if the only steps forward are to hire staff to be able to monitor and control this risk. For large organizations with thousands, if not tens of thousands, of devices to monitor, then the answer is yes dedicated staff may be required. However, in organizations where the monitoring is in the tens to hundreds of devices, then the answer would be no; hiring full-time staff is not a necessity. How, then can this be accomplished for your firm? Knowing that access to the tools and expertise to internally manage these risks is cost prohibitive for smaller organizations, how can an RIA firm the size of yours attain the needed level of security-based monitoring, remediation, and reaction to threats? If the amount of expectable change is proportional to the size of your organization; then the amount of data generated when monitoring your organization's network and devices will be smaller and more manageable. Likewise, the findings incurred by ongoing monitoring will be more manageable. Key factors like these open the door to the use of third party security service providers. A Managed Security Service Provider (or MSSP) is an outsourced service provider which provides a systematic approach to deploying and managing cyber security solutions to meet your organization's needs.

A properly equipped MSSP would be able to provide a vast toolset of services at either an a la carte or subscription basis level to meet your business' needs. Such services may include:

- Security Policy and Procedure Consulting

- Penetration and Vulnerability Testing

- Managed Security and Vulnerability Monitoring

- Compliance Testing and Monitoring

- Incident Response

The goals for your firm being:

- to establish secure computing standards

- to develop a secure baseline for your computing environment

- ongoing monitoring to maintain security and the ability to react to risks

Red Flag - I have a firewall on my network and antivirus installed on each desktop, isn't that enough to take care of cyber security?

Having a firewall and antivirus installed are the base requirement needed when considering the security of your network. However, these two factors can essentially be compared to locking your doors and windows and arming your alarm system on your home. Both are a good start, but don't begin to cover all the aspects by which your network, like your home, can be attacked and compromised.

Firewalls are software or devices that give a systems administrator the ability to allow and/or deny traffic into a particular system within the network. Configuration steps are taken and define these rules of where network traffic is allowed go. Your firewall would allow email, from the Internet, to flow into and out of your email server; while it denies most other traffic, from the Internet, access to the server at the same time. To properly configure network and software firewalls, a thorough analysis must be completed defining services provided by servers and which of the servers and services are available to each of your network segments. These approved access pathways are then set up to deny or block anything that was deemed acceptable traffic. Of course, this configuration needs to be maintained as changes to services, servers and access restrictions come up. A common point of failure in firewall configuration comes when new software is installed and cannot function properly because of a too restrictive firewall. Due to the urgency required to correct the issue, often the firewall's effectiveness is weakened in an effort to "quick fix" the software issue. Systems administrators are under pressure to make sure that the functionally, performance and availability of the network and its services are in place. Security tends to get pushed aside when something is broken and needs to be fixed "right now."

Antivirus software programs are installed on every computer within your network and strive to stop malicious programs and viruses from executing and doing damage. These Antivirus programs use two common methodologies for identifying suspicious programs. The most common and widely used method works through identifiable signatures. Every program possesses unique aspects which enable parts of the file to be stitched together into a distinct "fingerprint" or "signature" identifying the program. These signatures are considerably smaller than the whole program making managing large databases of millions of signatures feasible. These databases are commonly called "signatures" or "definitions." Every time a piece of malicious software is identified and tracked by the antivirus manufacturers, these signature databases are updated to remain current. This makes ensuring that your antivirus subscription is active and your definitions are up-to-date critical in making sure your antivirus is running at peak efficiency. The second methodology in use by some antivirus software is identification of malicious characteristic known as "heuristics." These antivirus products attempt to learn and identify patterns in a program's execution which are the telltale signs to malicious activity. This is much harder to do then to define. While the heuristics approach is becoming more and more reliable, it is still far from perfect and is usually paired with the signature based method for identifying malicious software.

The problem with these technologies is that given the ever-changing state of computers, networks, and software; your firewall and antivirus defense can go from pretty secure to "not so" secure at any given moment. If your firewall configuration is not properly maintained as you add, remove, or reconfigure devices within your network, the security provided by the firewall can fall short.

Likewise, antivirus applications can be easily bypassed by simply falling out of sync with their signatures or if an attacker uses one of a myriad of methods including non-publicly disclosed security bugs (zero-day bugs), the targeting of un-patched systems, or through the delivery of custom malware via email phishing attacks. Essentially, if the attack method of choice has not been seen before or the malicious activity behind the attack is delayed or disguised to appear benign, then your antivirus protection can be circumvented.

Augmenting these basic levels of system security with proactive security technologies such as real-time continuous threat scanning, periodic vulnerability scanning, and event correlation though log monitoring can help to fill the voids left simply by the deployment of a firewall and the installation of antivirus software. Running a networked environment without proper firewalling or antivirus protection would be highly ill advised; however, making an assumption that all bases are covered with the implementation of these two technologies alone falls short when attempting to deploy effective security measures and policy.

Red Flag – We have antivirus installed, so we should be safe from Crypto-Locker and other email based attacks, right?

Unfortunately Crypto-Locker and many other malicious programs are not always stopped by antivirus or antispyware programs. As described in the previous red flag, antivirus and anti-malware programs use either signature based identification or complex heuristics mechanisms to attempt to identify and stop malware before it can do its damage. One may think that the encryption of all your files should be an identifiable attack. Unfortunately, the application of encryption is a normal computing function; after all a legitimate user is logged in to the computer. This user downloaded and ran a program to encrypt all files. From a sheer logical perspective, the antivirus has no way of knowing if the user intended to run encryption software of not. Moreover, there are untold thousands of variants each with unique signatures already out there damaging files with hundreds if not thousands of new variants being readily deployed. Antivirus applications should be able to stop most of these versions that are identifiable by signature, but when all of your files are at risk, this is a far cry from effective protection.

The best defense against these types of malware is education, vigilance and effective backup and recovery policies. Spear-Phishing attacks are attacks against your network in which carefully crafted emails are delivered to employees of your firm with the intent of coercing the recipient into interacting with the message. The interaction can be as simple as clicking on a link within the email message or downloading and opening an attachment of the message. In either scenario, once the recipient complies with the attackers request for action, the malicious software is given opportunity to do its damage. When dealing with Spear-Phishing type emails, user education is paramount as a first line of defense. Recipients should always be familiar with who is sending them the email message and make an attempt to verify the email address rather than just look at the common name. The email address can be verified by looking at the "email address" portion on the "from:" line of the email:

From: John Smith <abc123@attacker.net>

In this example, regardless of whether you are familiar with John Smith, you should verify that his email address is correct. Moreover, one should never open an email's attachment unless there was an expectation of receiving attachments. If John Smith never sends you attached files nor were you expecting an attachment from John, extra care should be taken when dealing with the file or files that were received.

Given the social norm which email communications have become and how comfortable society is with using email programs as web browsers, even the most vigilant can succumb to malicious Spear-Phishing attacks. When this does happen, and it will, secondary systems need to be in place to identify the breach, contain the damage, and revert back to a pre-compromised state.

Red Flag - We really never change our passwords, I came up with a really good one back in 1996 and I'm sure no one can figure it out, right?

Password security is one of the most misunderstood and despised aspects of establishing effective systems and data security protocols. Passwords are typically considered to be a nuisance that, while limiting access to sensitive data, makes life more difficult for its owner on a daily basis.

Account credentials tend to be looked upon as the 'key' that is needed to unlock your computer, much like the key to your home. Unfortunately, unlike a physical key, you cannot retract your password once you have shared it with someone. What most people tend not to understand is that not only do these account credentials act as a 'key' but they come packaged with this perceived notion of identity. It is not just a 'key' to unlock something, it is YOU who has unlocked it; and all the rights YOU have on that website, computer or network is granted to YOU at login or to anyone who happens to login using YOUR credentials. While most people readily share their credentials with others for the sheer sake of convenience; they do so with little understanding of the bigger picture.

Due to the changes and advancements in computer technologies and how attacker's structure common attacks we always recommend that our clients implement a strong password policy. While it may seem daunting, our recommendation to clients is that passwords should be as long and complex as possible. Our personal preferences are that passwords be at least 15 characters long and include a minimum of one capital letter and one character symbol each at a random location within the password. Other important aspects of a good password policy are the frequency at which your passwords are changed and the limitation on the amount of failed attempts before the account is temporarily locked. Our recommendations on these points are that passwords be changed every 90 days and that accounts be locked for 5 minutes after 5 failed attempts.

With these recommendations we receive quite a bit of push back; after all passwords are rarely seen as anything other than a nuisance. We commonly hear arguments like, "You want me to tell everyone that they have to remember and type in a long fifteen plus character passwords. And that which they only have five attempts to get it right before they're locked out for five minutes. I had a hard enough of a time getting them to lock their screen when they stepped away from their computer." Unfortunately, yes these are our recommendations. The computer systems of today are becoming extremely powerful as are network speeds becoming faster. These advancements in technology work against the protections offered by simple password schemes.

Very common attacks against password systems are nothing more than customized passwords guessing exercises. And they are very effective. Depending on what is being attacked, attackers can setup automated systems with specially designed dictionaries consisting of hundreds of millions of password possibilities. These dictionaries take into account password norms such as letter for number substitutions, capitalization, word combinations, numbers appended to the ends of words (dates, years, etc.), special character placement, and so on. And more often than not, these dictionaries are customized for the attack using employee social media information (LinkedIn, Facebook, Twitter, etc.) and the company website. Given the speed of computers and networks hundreds if not thousands of username and password variations can be tested every minute for network based attacks. When hashed (or encrypted) passwords are stolen and tested offline, on the attacker's systems, millions if not billions of variations can be tested per second. To put this in perspective, given a seven character passwords there are roughly 70 trillion possible permutations in total. At one billion guesses per second, every single possible seven character password can be tested in less than twenty hours. When these attacks methods are correctly employed, it is all too common for a large percentage of the passwords to be recovered if password length, complexity, and account locking are not stressed.

New technologies striving to aid in solving these types of problem are Multi-Factor Authentication products. These are products that, when deployed, require a user to enter their username, password, and a random number generated by a device they have in their possession. This rides on the principal of authentication to a system based on "something secret" like your password and "something you have" as in a fob or device which generates temporary, unique and random numbers for the user. While not foolproof, these technologies greatly enhance the security of user authentication at a controllable price point.

Red Flag - Let me send you the excel file with all our usernames and passwords – then you'll see how secure they are, okay?

When malicious attackers compromise a computer system, one of the first things they seek is the system's stored passwords. One might wonder why someone would want something that gives them access to the system when they already have access to the system. The answer is simple, it is known as 'password reuse' and it is a common practice. When someone finally comes up with a password they feel is difficult enough, they memorize it and use it everywhere – the office, the internet, the bank's website, shopping sites, basically anywhere that a 'good' password is required. Malicious hackers know how common 'password reuse' is and by gaining access to passwords or stealing them, the hacker has most likely gained limitless access to so much more than that on system!

What does this mean to you? Well, securing passwords is a difficult task due to the social misunderstanding of password use and how passwords are most commonly attacked. Your firm's staff (and probably you too) needs to be trained to believe that every password is a secret of the utmost importance and should never be shared or reused. If it must be shared, for technician access or a similar circumstance, it should be changed immediately following the event. Since creating and remembering multiple secure passwords is next to impossible, a specially designed password keeper/vault software should be used to both generate and store your passwords.

Shared accounts should be avoided if possible; but if not, the appropriate tools for managing shared secrets should be utilized to keep passwords secure and to facilitate ease when the password must be changed.

When considering how to keep your secret passwords truly secret, we would recommend the following:

- **Each user should be the only person who knows their password** - corporate policy should state that no employee should ever share their password with anyone - not even their supervisors or management.

- **The only mechanism for storing passwords should be password keeper/vault software for each individual user or a specially designed product for sharing**

group secrets where shared credentials are required. An Excel, Word, Text, or Note file should never be created to store passwords - by any individual and for any reason.

- **Password strength can be determined by specially trained security professionals during a password audit** – in this type of audit hashed passwords (a process similar to encryption but used with passwords) are attacked in an attempt to retrieve the clear text form for as many passwords as possible. The results of this audit describe password patterns in use, strengths and weaknesses, resilience to attack, and other key factors that should be addressed within the organization password policy and employee training methodologies. This type of audit should completed only by specially trained professionals with the understanding that some if not all of the hashed passwords maybe compromised thus will require password changes.

Red Flag - Everyone has administrative rights on their desktops; it just makes everything so much easier, don't you think?

Administrative rights to a computer give that user full and absolute control over that specific machine. They have the ability to install and remove software, start and stop services, add and remove other local accounts, read or write to almost every file within the system, and so much more. Many times local admin is granted to users to allow them to install the programs they may need to do their daily job functions. While yes, allowing your employees to install their own applications might seem efficient for the few times they may need to add approved software to their computers, but the risks far outweigh the efficiencies.

The fact of the matter is while at times employees do find themselves needing the installation of an approved software package, more often than not the software being installed is not approved for use and just something the employee would like to try out to gauge its usefulness. This is most likely free software downloaded from a random website; that may be used once and then forgotten. These points introduce considerable risk to you as a business owner. If the software being installed was downloaded from an internet file sharing site, it may be illegally unlocked and you may be liable for running unlicensed software. Likewise, many internet file sharing sites are known to have malicious versions of software. You install the software which you intended but received a bonus malware package as part of the deal. As for single use applications which are installed and forgotten; many remote access exploits are introduced into systems when rarely used software goes unpatched and is left running on a system. The fact of the matter is the need to control a system at an administrative level should not occur often. When the need does arise appropriate systems administrative staff should be the ones making changes to the system and ensuring that system plays by the rules and functions which are appropriate within the network.

A greater risk factor with standing local admin rights is that majority of today's attacks on a system occur at the client or should I say at the workstation. This means your users and their computers are being attacked; be it through malicious email attacks, such as Spear-Phishing, or the accidental browsing of a malicious website. The fact is, more often than not, a compromise of your network will originate on a user's workstation. When this happens and the user has local administrative rights, the attacker will be granted those same privileges. This ultimately grants your malicious visitor the ability to install the tools of their trade and escalate attacks with the full permissions on that computer. The attacker will unquestionably use local admin rights to attack stored network/domain credentials to gain a foothold on the compromised computer as well as onto other network resources.

Many times we hear arguments that "it's only local admin on the workstation and not admin on the domain or network." This is a flawed assumption. Having the ability to fully control a networked computer is a very powerful position; regardless of whether local admin grants network resource access or not. The ability to escalate from local admin to network access is not a hacking skill deemed difficult or one only employed by hacker elite. Simple escalation from local admin to network access is a very real risk and one that should not be weighed lightly when deciding if the added "ease" of providing local administrative rights is warranted.

Red Flag - We were hit by the Crypto-Locker malware and all of my files were lost, should I just pay the ransom?

We advise against paying any fees to any 'ransom-ware' programs like Crypto-Locker. First, you will be inadvertently aiding the proliferation of these types of malicious software attacks. Second, there is a high probability that payment will not be successful. At the writing of this book, the United Stated Department of Justice, in conjunction with the FBI and other international law enforcement agencies, have been successfully dismantling the control server network used to control the CryptoLocker malware, effectively neutralizing this particular threat. If you have been effected by CryptoLocker there is a chance you may be able to restore your data. Based on information collected by security research firms Fox-IT and FireEye a substantial quantity of encryption keys have been discovered. These keys may work for decrypting your CryptoLocker encrypted files. A website located at https://www.decryptcryptolocker.com/ can test one of your encrypted files to see if there is an available key with which decryption can be completed.

ītegrîa

VI. IT for RIA's with Integrity - ĪTEGRIA™?

ĪTEGRIA™ is the brainchild of Richard Mabbun and Julian Makas that arose from a desire to solve a problem they saw in the IT Industry. The problem was with IT in general, but specifically related to IT solutions that are available to small to medium sized businesses. The first problem is there is essentially no one taking responsibility for the IT solutions they are promising to deliver. The second problem is when the solution is not delivered, no one is accountable. And lastly, IT solutions tend not to be in the best interest of the client.

ÎTEGRIA™ means to solve those problems by delivering the IT solutions that small to medium size RIA firms need to meet the needs of their clients and be competitive in the marketplace. Here's how it happens.

ÎTEGRIA™ fills the need in small to medium RIA firms that an internal IT department would if the RIA firm were able to afford or staff one, and they do it with responsibility, accountability and service. ÎTEGRIA™ has created a service model that takes protecting their clients seriously by taking up the task to provide incredible technology, excellent service and unmatched security in the continually evolving threat landscape that exist today. The team at ÎTEGRIA™ truly loves technology and service and the challenges that threats to your company bring; knowing that technology and service can be done well (just like the mega-businesses) even in smaller firms.

When we imagined ÎTEGRIA™, one of their main goals was to provide true customer service to their clients.

Let's face it, customer service rarely exist in this day and age because the customer service representatives are representing the company who pays them and not the customer who needs their service. With ĪTEGRIA™, you and your firm should expect something completely different because that is the way ĪTEGRIA™ promises it will be. A call to customer service at ĪTEGRIA™ connects you with the person who knows you, your company, and your system; you'll find no "did you turn on your PC?" questions here, but instead a real live person who is ready to help you right away!

ĪTEGRIA™ came into existence to provide small to medium size RIA firms with IT solutions delivered with responsibility, accountability and a superior level of customer service. To ĪTEGRIA™ customer services is defined by taking care of your firm's needs and ensuring that everything is always operating at the highest possible level. It is a promise to provide you with **service in your best interest** and accountability and responsibility at the same high level; because honestly, the growth of your RIA firm means the growth of ĪTEGRIA™.

You are now acquainted with ĪTEGRIA™'s goals, but let's explore what you came here for – IT solutions and security. Cyber security, as you know, is highly specialized, as well as resource and time sensitive. This is the point where it becomes convoluted and begins to appear that large businesses have an unfair edge. The truth is, security is a necessity, no matter the size of your firm. You need it just like you need telephone and internet services to conduct your business every single day.

Now, you are probably thinking, this is going to cost way more than my RIA firm can afford, just by the service promise alone and not even including the actual security. In reality, many small to medium size firms feel this way - security is a necessity that is completely out of reach. Here is where ĪTEGRIA™ comes in – Security can be expensive and determining what your needs are takes a lot of time. Even if you have time to do the research, you may feel you need an IT professional to explain it all to you. At ĪTEGRIA™ we offer small to medium size businesses a blended rate/time assured service that allows us to distribute what is often a high-priced cost load among many smaller firms to bring service to all. It is the service you picture in a business with 50,000 plus computers but not in a small to medium size RIA firm with 5 to 20 computers. At ĪTEGRIA™, we want to change that picture by delivering network and technology assessments that focus on the security needs of your distinct business.

ĪTEGRIA™ focuses on technology and security that is RIA firm specific. It is all we do – provide RIA firms, just like yours, with customized services, solutions and security designed to protect your business – after all – the financial services industry is the target of the shrewdest hackers. Because of our focus on this sector of the industry, we understand your challenges as well as your technology needs and we promise to deliver exactly what you need with responsibility, accountability and service in your best interest.

Review your RIA Networks

We hope that you can use this book and its Red Flags to investigate the networks and technology at your RIA firm. Dig deeper and ask your IT Support firm about your Backups, Disaster Recovery, IT Compliance, and Cyber Security. Use the questions from each Red Flag as a starting point and see what answers you receive. Are the answers consistent with ĪTEGRIA™'s?

Notes

Made in the USA
San Bernardino, CA
04 March 2015